FROM THE FARM TO THE TABLE HEALTHY FOODS FROM THE FARM FOR KIDS CHILDREN'S AGRICULTURE BOOKS

BABY PROFESSOR

EDUCATION KIDS

Speedy Publishing LLC
40 E. Main St. #1156
Newark, DE 19711
www.speedypublishing.com

Teaching kids to eat healthy foods will help them develop healthy eating patterns in life.

Milk is rich in calcium. Calcium is important for strong and healthy bones.

Cheese is made from milk. The milk of cows and goats are the most popular.

Butter is also a dairy food product. Butter is usually made from cow's milk. Butter is used as a substitute for oil when cooking.

Eggs are rich in protein. Protein replaces and maintains the tissues in our bodies.

Chicken is also rich in protein and has low amounts of fat. Chicken is also rich in vitamin B3 which helps with our metabolism.

Beef is rich in nutrients. Beef is rich in Protein and Zinc. Zinc helps create a healthy immune system.

Pork is rich in protein and minerals. A moderate consumption of pork makes an excellent addition to a healthy diet.

Broccoli is rich in Potassium and and Vitamin A. Potassium helps our heart and muscles work better.

Eggplant is a good source of dietary fibers, Vitamins C and K. Fiber helps prevent constipation.

Cabbage is also rich in fiber and cholesterol free. Cabbage is also a good source of Calcium and Vitamin C.

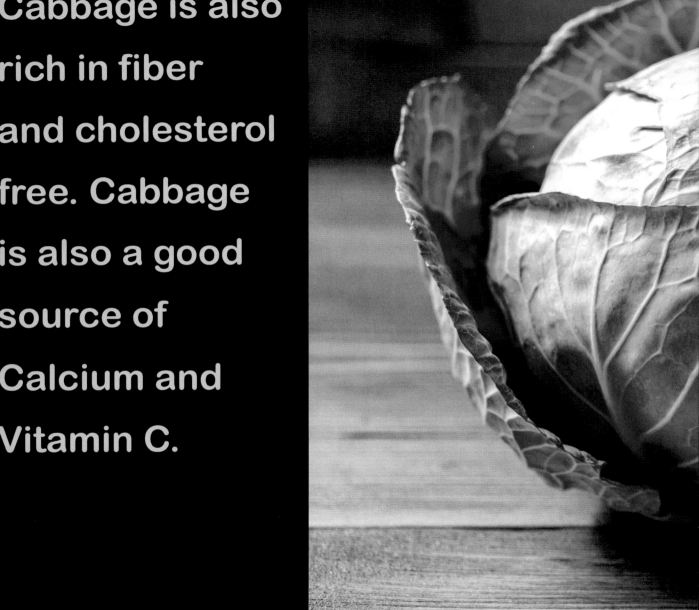

Cauliflower is an excellent source of vitamin C. You can eat it raw to retain all the vitamins.

Tomato is rich in lycopene, which is good for the heart and helps fight cancer.

Carrots are rich in beta-carotene.Beta-carotene is important for our eyesight and skin health.

Cucumbers have lots of Vitamin C. Cucumbers are also rich in B vitamins which gives us energy.

Grapes are a good source of Vitamin C and dietary fiber. Grape skins are also rich in antioxidants.

An Apple is an excellent source of fiber which reduces blood cholesterol and helps build healthy bodies.

An Orange is rich in Vitamin C which helps the growth and repair of tissues in our body.

Eating healthy foods is important especially for children to have a healthy body and an active mind.

Visit

BABY PROFESSOR
EDUCATION KIDS

www.BabyProfessorBooks.com

to download Free Baby Professor eBooks
and view our catalog of new and exciting
Children's Books

Made in the USA
Las Vegas, NV
02 June 2024

90617779R00026